The Busy Housewife

Luke 15: God Rescues

CATHERINE MACKENZIE
Illustrated by Chiara Bertelli

When you lose something precious, you look for it and look for it. You want to get it back. If you lose something big – it can be easier to find than something small.

If you lose something that moves and makes a noise it can be easier to find than something that is still and quiet.

   If you lose something precious and tiny, that doesn't move and makes no sound, it can be very hard to find.

Jesus told a story about a housewife who had ten precious coins. One day she lost one. What a disaster! The coin was valuable. She longed to get it back, so she went to work.

Light was needed, so she lit a lamp. The floor was dusty, so she got her broom. Soon she had begun to sweep the whole house.

After a lot of searching she finally found the missing coin.

The tiny, precious, silent coin was sitting in a corner, almost unseen. The housewife found it and was so happy.

She was so happy in fact, that she went out and called all her friends and neighbours together for a party. 'Rejoice with me for I have found my lost coin!'

Jesus said, 'It's just like this in heaven when a sinner is sorry for their sin and turns to God. There is great joy!' Every lost sinner who comes to God causes a great celebration in heaven.

What does Jesus want us to learn from this story? Well, he wants us to realise that sinners are like coins. We are valuable. More valuable than the coins in your piggy bank. More valuable than the jewels on your mother's dresser. God loves us.

We are so valuable that God sent his Son, Jesus Christ, to this world to suffer and die to save sinners.

But a lost coin or a missing ring can't help its owner to find it. We can't help God to save us. It's only God that saves. The coin couldn't move. The coin couldn't speak. The coin didn't even know it was lost.

We can't say or do anything to save us from sin. Until God changes us we don't even know that we're sinners and need God's help.

Lost sinners are like the coin, so that means God is like the housewife. She worked hard to find the coin and didn't give up. God doesn't give up either. He has done everything that's needed to save sinners. He sent Jesus. He gives us his Word, the Bible, and his Holy Spirit helps us understand it.

WHO IS THE HOLY SPIRIT? God is one God in three persons: God the Father, God the Son and God the Holy Spirit. They save sinners together. God sent Jesus to save. Jesus gave up his life to save and the Holy Spirit changes you inside. One day those who trust in God will be sinless like Jesus.

When you trust in Jesus you can't be proud. You can't say, 'God has saved me because I'm so good and great and I deserve it.' Nobody deserves any of God's goodness. God saves because he is a loving God, full of mercy.

So if lost sinners are like the lost coin, and God is like the busy housewife who is like the lamp and the broom?

The lamp and the broom are like the people who love God. God uses people to find lost sinners. How can God use you? What can you do? You can pray to God for people who do not love him.

You can tell others about God's love. You can show others what God is like by obeying him and being like him. In everything you do you can show others how great God is.

God wants his people to work with him. He wants them to love lost sinners as he does. He wants them to be joyful whenever a lost sinner is saved from sin.

If you haven't trusted in Jesus you are lost, like the coin. There is nothing you can do by yourself to save yourself from this danger. It is only God who can change you. It is only God who can save you.

If you trust in Jesus you are found. God did this! He is amazing. Thank him for his love and praise him for his power.

Every lost sinner is valuable. God is happy when sinners are found. We must tell others about how loving God is.

We should rejoice whenever God saves.

Christian Focus Publications

Christian Focus Publications publishes books for adults and children under its four main imprints: Christian Focus, CF4K, Mentor and Christian Heritage. Our books reflect our conviction that God's Word is reliable and Jesus is the way to know him, and live for ever with him. Our children's list includes a Sunday School curriculum that covers pre-school to early teens, and puzzle and activity books. We also publish personal and family devotional titles, biographies and inspirational stories that children will love. If you are looking for quality Bible teaching for children then we have an excellent range of Bible stories and age-specific theological books. From pre-school board books to teenage apologetics, we have it covered!

AUTHOR'S DEDICATON: To my friends and family at Kingsview Christian Centre, A.P.C.

10 9 8 7 6 5 4 3 2 1
Copyright © 2017 Catherine Mackenzie
ISBN: 978-1-5271-0092-3
Published in 2017 by Christian Focus Publications Ltd.
Geanies House, Fearn, Tain, Ross-shire, IV20 1TW, Great Britain
Illustrations by Chiara Bertelli
Cover Design: Sarah Korvemaker
Printed in Malta